GHASTLY JOKES

by Al Jaffee

Publishers · GROSSET & DUNLAP · New York
A FILMWAYS COMPANY

Library of Congress Catalog Card Number: 76-27263

ISBN: 0-448-12870-5 (Trade Edition)
ISBN: 0-448-13412-8 (Library Edition)

I eat my peas with honey,
I have done it all my life;
They do taste kind of funny,
But it keeps them on the knife.

There was a young man of Devizes
Whose ears were of different sizes.
   The one that was small
   Was of no use of all,
But the other won several prizes.

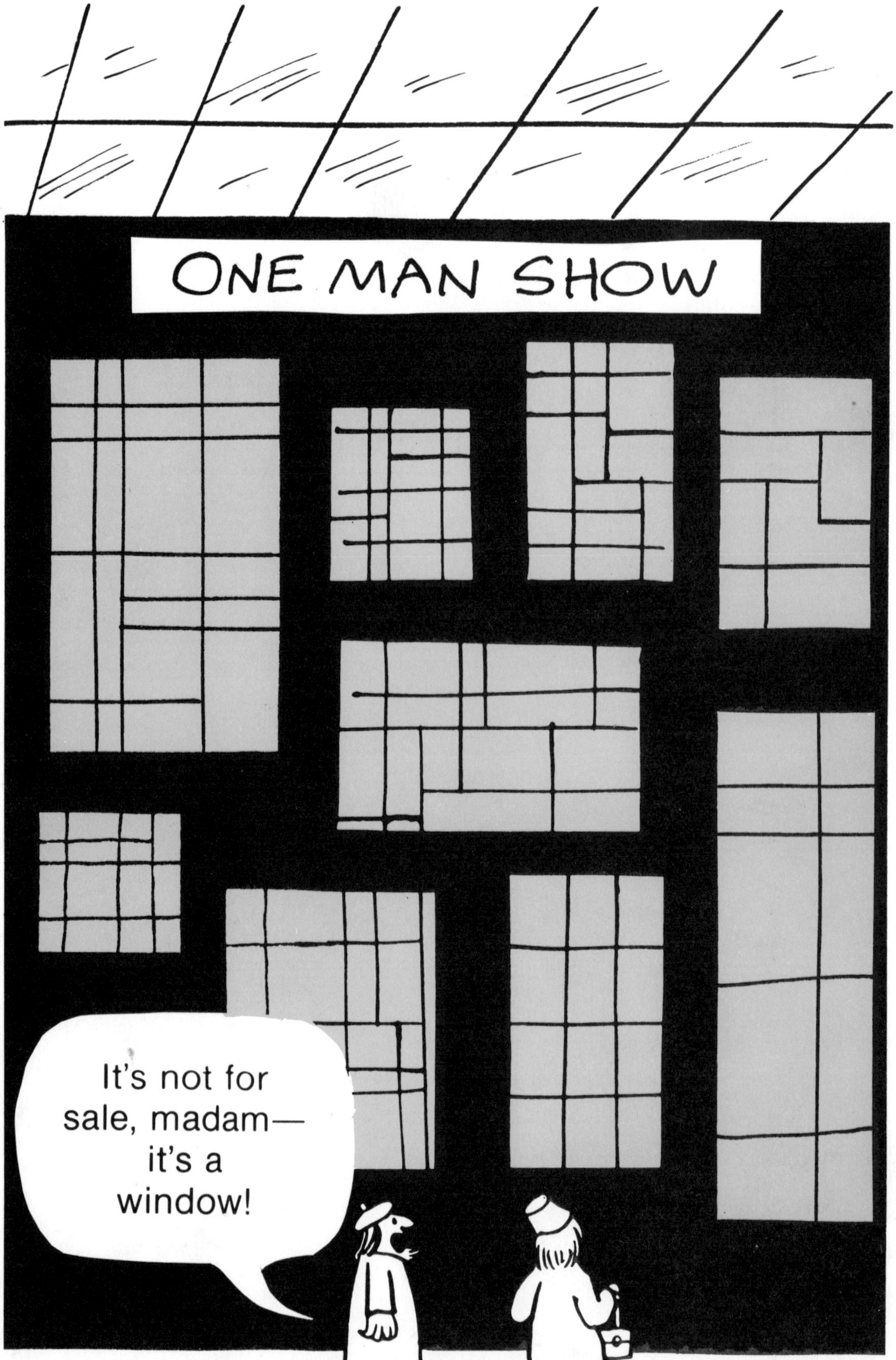
ONE MAN SHOW
It's not for sale, madam— it's a window!

DINER: Take this steak back at once! I've been trying to cut it for ten minutes, but it's so tough I can't even make a dent in it.

WAITER: I'm sorry, sir, but I can't take it back—you've bent it.

WAITRESS: Do you want your eggs turned over?

DINER: Yes, turn them over to the Museum of Natural History.

DINER: What are these pennies doing in my soup?

WAITER: Well, madam, you said you'd stop eating here if there wasn't some change in your meals.

WAITER: Sir, we're famous for snails here.
DINER: I thought so. I've been served by one already.

MOTHER: Jimmy's teacher says he ought to have an encyclopedia.
FATHER: Aw, let him walk to school like I did!

TEACHER: Why are you shivering, Albert?
ALBERT: It must be this zero on my test paper.

TEACHER: Name six animals of the arctic region.
PUPIL: Three walruses and three polar bears.

Melvin was caught cheating in astronomy class. The teacher asked him to describe the stars and he began hitting himself on the head.

SCIENCE TEACHER: The light from the sun comes to us at a speed of approximately 186,000 miles per second.
STUDENT: Yeah, but it's all downhill.

CALLER: Doctor, come at once! Our baby has swallowed a ball-point pen.

DOCTOR: I'll be right over. What are you doing in the meantime?

CALLER: Using a pencil.

PATIENT: I'm having trouble with my breathing.

DOCTOR: I see. Well, I can give you something to stop that.

HARRY: If a lion were stalking you, what steps would you take?
BARRY: The longest steps I could.

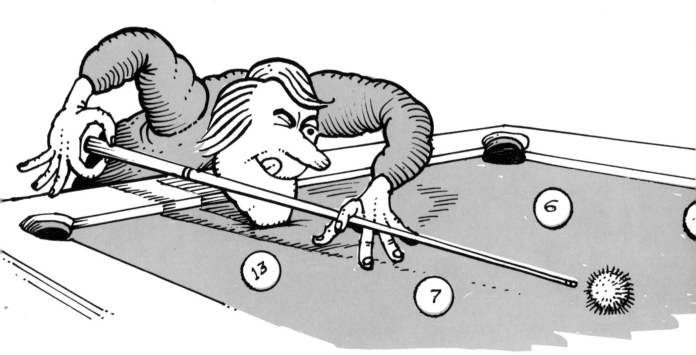

A chemist once mixed a solution that could put hair on a billiard ball, but it gained him no wealth at all. No one wanted to buy a billiard ball with hair on it.

KIM: If you were going through the woods, would you rather have a lion eat you or a bear?

TIM: I'd rather have the lion eat the bear.

CHUCK: What's the best thing to put into a pie?

CHRIS: Your teeth.

How do you spell "mousetrap" in three letters?
C-A-T.

How do you make a slow horse fast?
Don't give him anything to eat for a while.

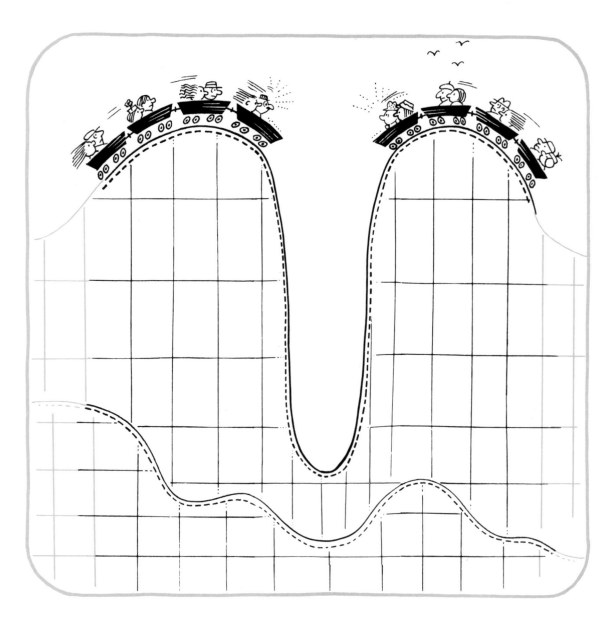

1.

It's a ticket
for going through
a "stop" sign.

2.

JOE: I'll have you know that everyone in my block looks to me for advice and follows it.

FLO: I don't doubt it. You're a natural-born blockhead.

OLD HEN: Let me give you some advice.

YOUNG HEN: Yes, what is it?

OLD HEN: An egg a day keeps the ax away.

SALLY: Why don't you buy Christmas seals?
SILLY: Oh, I really don't know how I'd feed them!

MAID (to Lady of the House): While you were gone, ma'am, your little son swallowed a bug. But don't worry—I sprayed him with insect poison.

FIRST JAILBREAKER: I wonder why the bloodhounds aren't trailing us.
SECOND JAILBREAKER: I threw a penny in the stream and they followed the cent.

BOSS: Did you put that note where it would be sure to attract Mr. Webb's attention when he came in?

OFFICE BOY: Yes—I stuck a pin through it and put it on his chair.

A visitor from the city was watching a farmer going about his planting.

"I guess I don't know about such things," said the city man, "so would you mind telling me why you mix onions with your potatoes?"

"Well," was the farmer's explanation, "the onions will make the potatoes' eyes water and I won't have to worry about a dry spell."

SHOPPER: Don't you think that these eggs are rather small?
STOREKEEPER: Yes, I do. That's the trouble with the farmers. They're so anxious to sell their eggs, they take them out of the nest too soon.

BAKERY CLERK: Here's a very nice cake—I'm sure you'll like it.
CUSTOMER: Umm-m, I don't know. That cake looks as if the mice had been eating it.
BAKERY CLERK: Impossible. The cat has been lying on it all night.

MRS. HOMEBODY: I sent my little boy over to get two pounds of butter cookies and you only sent me a pound and a half. Something must be wrong with your scales.
STOREKEEPER: My scales are all right, Mrs. Homebody. Have you weighed your little boy?

DINER: I would like a cup of coffee and a muttered buffin.
WAITER: You mean a buffered muttin, don't you?
DINER: No, I mean a muffered buttin.
WAITER: Wouldn't you like some doughnuts and milk?

BILLY: That fellow over there is handicapped with an eye disorder. Everything he looks at, he sees double.

TILLIE: Poor man! I imagine he must find it hard to get a job.

BILLY: No—the gas and electric company hired him to read meters.

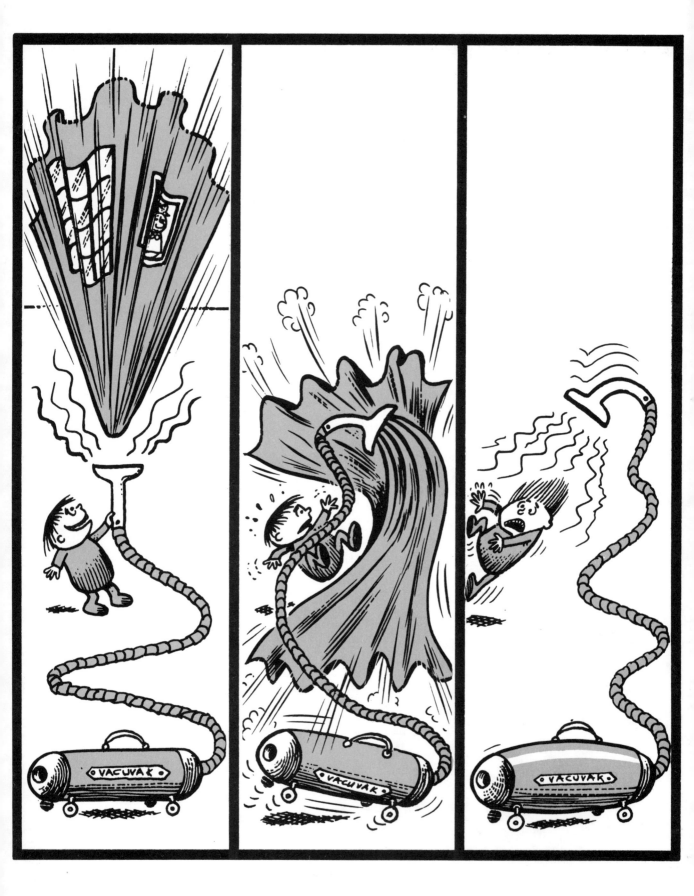

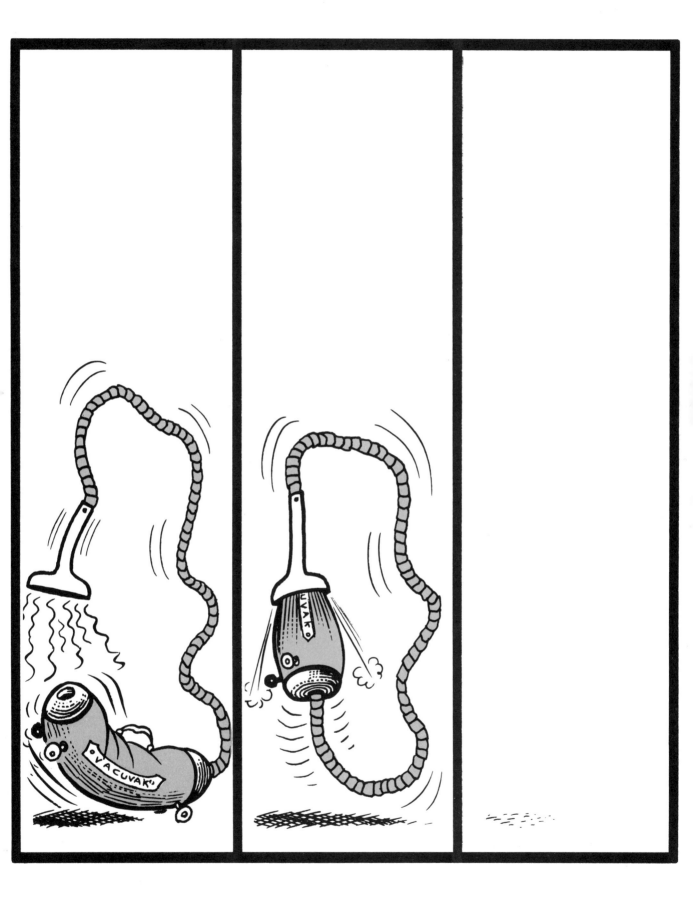

FARMER: Where's that mule I told you to take out and have shod?
HIRED HAND: Oh, did you say *shod?* I thought you said *shot!*

ARTY: Look at that bunch of cows.
SMARTY: Not bunch—"herd."
ARTY: Heard what?
SMARTY: Herd of cows.
ARTY: Sure, I've heard of cows.
SMARTY: I mean a cowherd.
ARTY: Well, what do I care if a cow heard? I didn't say anything I shouldn't have!

WHEELER: That horse you sold me is a fine animal, but I can't get him to hold his head up.

DEALER: Well, that's because of his pride. He'll hold it up as soon as he's paid for.

BEN: It's a funny thing—all dogs, no matter how vicious, will come up to me and lick my hand.

KEN: Maybe if you'd eat with a knife and fork, they wouldn't be so friendly.

POST OFFICE CLERK: Is this package for you? The name is obliterated.

MAN: No, that can't be mine. My name is O'Brien.

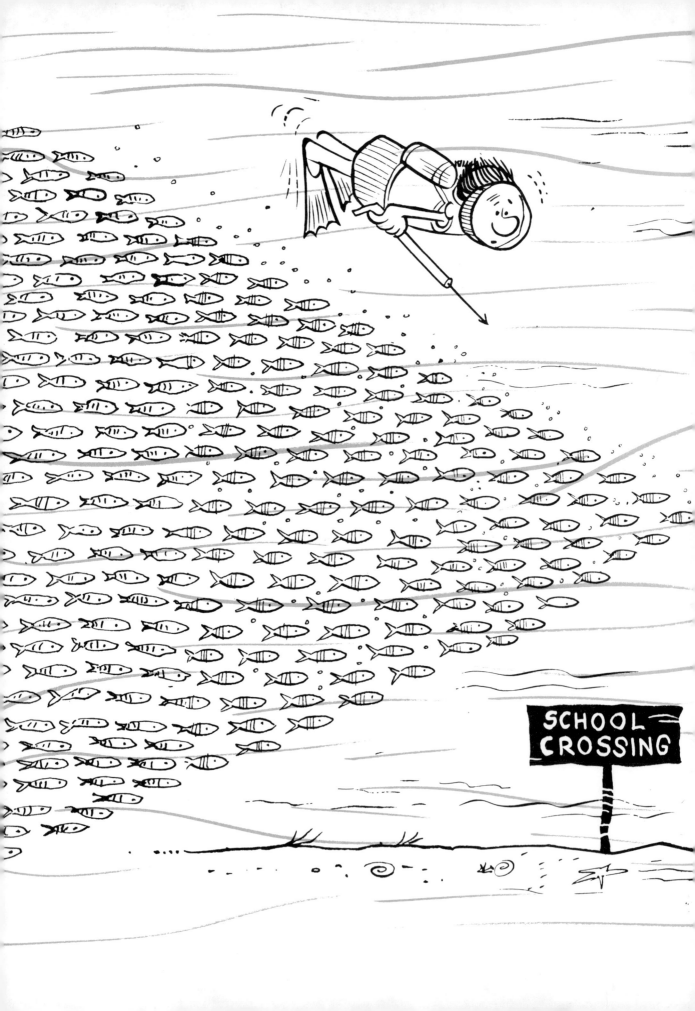

Hickory, dickory, dock,
Two mice ran up the clock,
The clock struck one,
But the other one got away.

NIT: Gee, I can't make up my mind whether I should ask Kate or Edith to be my wife.

WIT: Well, you can't have your Kate and Edith, too!

VIC: The house I'm moving into is right by a railroad station.

QUICK: Won't that disturb your sleep?

VIC: No. They say I can get used to it in a few nights, so for the first week or so I'll sleep in a hotel.

There was a young fellow named Hall
Who fell in the spring in the fall.
   'Twould have been a sad thing
   If he died in the spring,
But he didn't—he died in the fall.

PATIENT: I called to make an appointment with the dentist.
NURSE: Dr. Braude is out at the moment.
PATIENT: Oh? When do you expect him to be out again?

PAUL: I once had to live on a can of beans for a whole week.
MIKE: My goodness! Weren't you afraid of falling off?

MOTORIST: Can you tell me how to get to Riversburg from here?

FARMER: Well, go back a couple of miles and take the first road to the left. No, maybe it's the second road to the left. Come to think of it, stranger, if I were trying to get to Riversburg, I wouldn't start from here at all.

ARCHIE: This dog must be a good watchdog.

ANDY: How do you know?

ARCHIE: He's so full of ticks.

EXPLORER: I was once stranded on an island and on the verge of starvation. I eventually became so hungry that I dined off my pet parrot.

LISTENER: What did it taste like?

EXPLORER: Oh, turkey, chicken, goose, wild duck—that bird could imitate anything!

JUDGE: The charges against you are that you ran over this man—and, also, speeding.

MOTORIST: Yes, your Honor—I was hurrying to get over him.

GARY: I wonder why that clock is slow.

LARRY: You'd be slow, too, if you had to run all day.

Why didn't the baseball catcher meet Cinderella?
Because he missed the ball.

Why is a baseball park cool?
Because there's a fan in every seat.

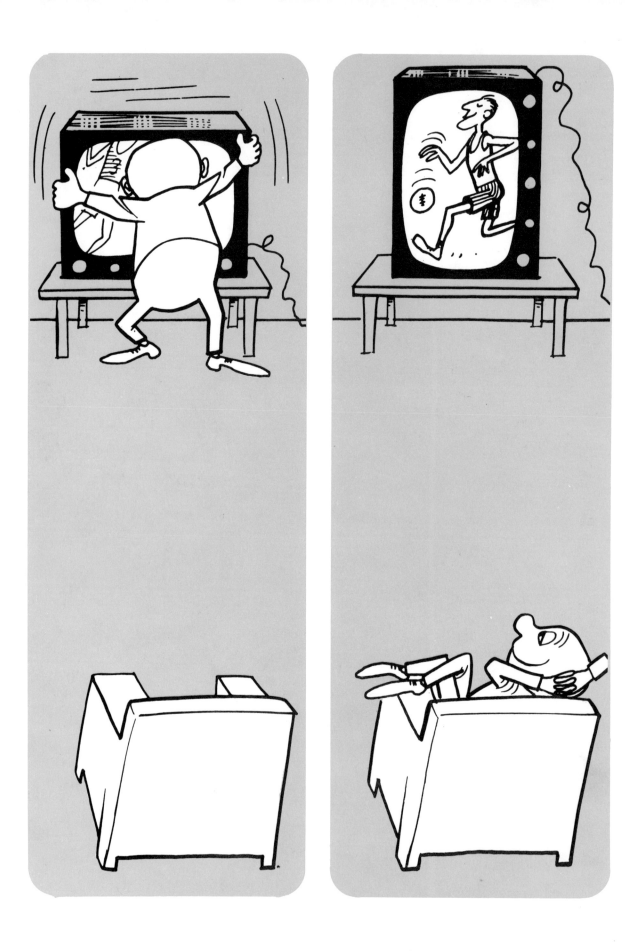

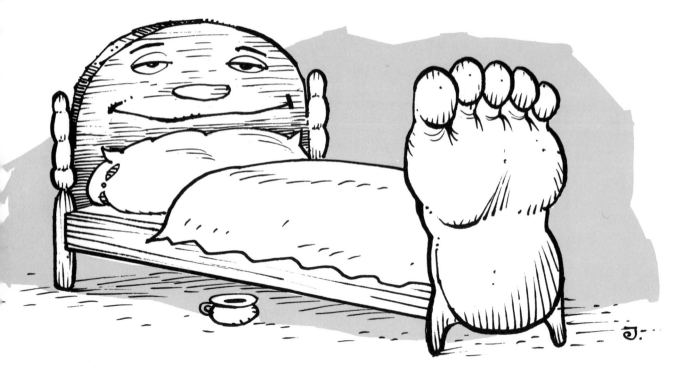

I have four legs, yet only one foot. What am I?
A bed.

Why is an island like the letter T?
Because it's in the middle of water.

MOTHER: Tommy, why did you put a frog in your little sister's bed?
TOMMY: Because I couldn't catch a mouse.

A very young girl—call her Emma—
Was seized with a terrible tremor.
  She had swallowed a spider
  Which stung her inside her—
Gadzooks, what an awful dilemma!

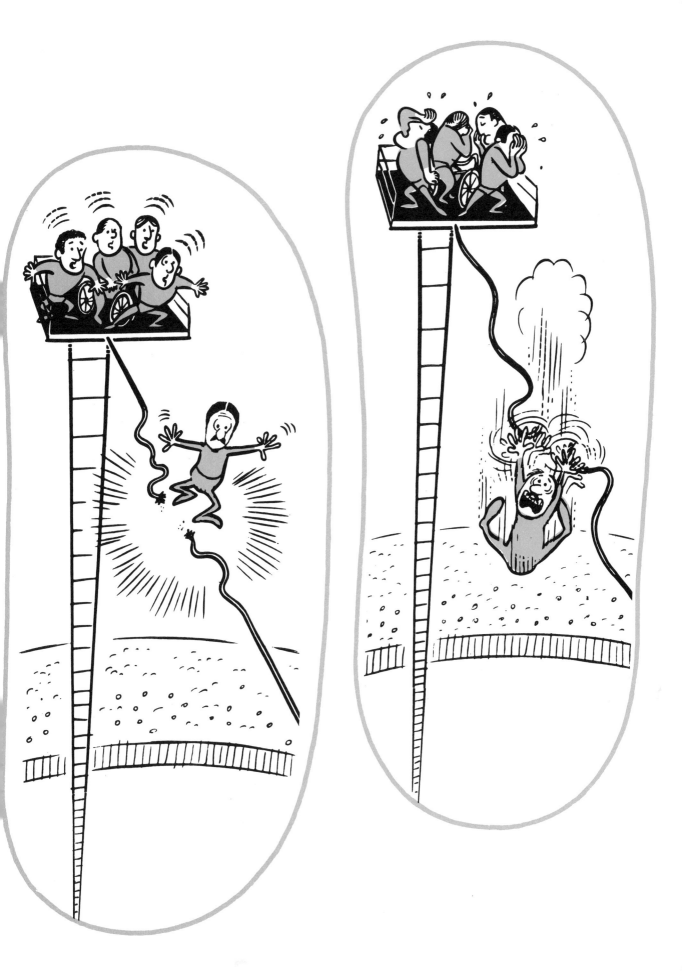

Why is a heart like a policeman?
It has a regular beat.

Why would a spider make a good outfielder?
Because it catches flies.

Why are clouds like people riding horses?
Because they hold the rains.

Why was the little strawberry worried?
Because his mother and father were in a jam.

AUNT MARTHA: And what are you going to give your baby brother for Christmas, Billy?

BILLY: I don't know. I gave him the measles last Christmas.

RAY: Do you like codfish balls?
KAY: I don't know—I've never been to one.

HENNY: Did you put new water in the fish bowl?
PENNY: I didn't have to. The fish haven't drunk what was in it yet.